Dear Blood,

poems

Carine Topal

BenYehuda Press
Teaneck, New Jersey

DEAR BLOOD, © 2025 Carine Topal. All rights reserved. No part of this book may be used or reproduced in any manner whatsoever without written permission except in the case of brief quotations embodied in critical articles and reviews.

Published by Ben Yehuda Press
122 Ayers Court #1B
Teaneck, NJ 07666

http://www.BenYehudaPress.com

To subscribe to our monthly book club and support independent Jewish publishing, visit https://www.patreon.com/BenYehudaPress

Jewish Poetry Project #54   http://jpoetry.us

978-1-963475-73-9 pb

Cover illustration: Rita Valles Woodward

25 26 27 / 10 9 8 7 6 5 4 3 2 1   20250109

Also by Carine Topal

POETRY COLLECTIONS

God as Thief
Bed of Want
In the Heaven of Never Before
Tattooed
In Order of Disappearance

ACKNOWLEDGEMENTS

Some of these poems first appeared in the following journals, with thanks to the editors.

Wet Grain, (UK): "There's Still the Fruit" and "Inventories"
Valparaiso Review: "Black Sea Port, 1941"
Caliban (online): "Ancient Fall"
Rhino: "Mother of Rough Tongue"
Three Elements Review: "Gleaned"
Naugatuck River Review: "A Lamenting"
Lily Poetry Review: "Threadbare, We are Homesick"
American Poetry Journal: "Kinship"
Spillway: "Teutophobia"
Westchester Review: "Elegy: Rehovot, Israel, 1984"
The Jewish Literary Journal: "Dear Blood,"
Furious Pure 003: "Gleaned" and "Ancient Fall"
Anacapa Review: "{The Crows of Dresden}"
Levure Litteraire: "Chagall Psalm"
International Literary Quarterly (Interlitq:) "My Father, Who Refused to Sit Shiva"
Pedestal: "Belye Nochi"

*In memory of my parents and brothers
And for my granddaughters, Shoshana and Daria*

*Let it come
like wildflowers,
suddenly, because the field
must have it: wildpeace.*

—Yehuda Amichai, from "Wildpeace"

Contents

I.

Inventories / 2
My Dead / 3
Chagall Psalm / 4
Kinship / 5
Belye Nochi / 6
Teutophobia / 7
Estrangement—like sacrifice—begins as a word at first, / 8
Black Sea Port, 1941 / 9
My Father, Who Refused to Sit Shiva / 10
Elegy: Rehovot, Israel, 1984 / 11
{The Crows of Dresden} / 12
Mother of Rough Tongue / 13
Gleaned / 14
A Lamenting / 15

II.

Ancient Fall / 18
There's Still the Fruit / 19
Threadbare, We are Homesick / 20
This Season / 21
A Field Guide to Oświęcim, 2012 / 23
They Filled with Promise and Worth / 24
If the muzzle of indifference / 25
Invocation / 26
A River / 27

Epilogue

Dear Blood, / 30

Notes / 32
About the Author / 33

I.

Inventories

A chipped cup half-filled with cherry jam.
    A clawed-out fruit fallen from a tree.
A tin box of mints. A girl named Sadie.
    Under her crinoline: love's blindness.
In the suburbs of my youth: the purple-marrowed brothers born before me.
    Within the closed-mouth matryoshka: a lungful of heartwood.
Chiseled in stone: my father, hunched in the same sun as his buried boys.
    In the shadows: my mother, mourning and half-crazed.
On the tip of Chagall's tongue: goats in the tree. Umbrellas
    looking calmly away.
On my tongue: milk still warm from the milking.
    Hidden in the hull of a ship: unnamed children leaning toward shore.

My Dead

  My dead are always   behind me

lingering in the   slow hereafter

My dead   who forget   how to wonder

who put me in charge   of the joy

               I who was once so young

My dead   my disfigured

and bound   my beloveds

lingering

  in the slow   hereafter

Chagall Psalm

For it was moonlight
in your town of old Jews
the quiet lunatic who
seeking paradise
drowned in the river
of his last winter

It was the tremors of childhood
through which you barely slept
a bed by a window looking
out to the near end of Yiddish
ash spewing from chimneys
the heat before the fire

It was *Shemah* for your mother who carried
the fever of a great loss
a sister hastily named Miriam
her heart chambers closed in the bright
sleeves of snow

Moysey, think of the rows of amber-roofed
homes pitched toward the banks
of your frozen river
the viridian run
of the Luchesa
the fires before you ran

Kinship

From the hum of the heatwave famine grows. River blindness is everywhere. The oncoming light brings no democracy. As if the looting and limping and turning away could loosen the earth and fatten our bellies. Birds chirp and caw. The draft horse with hooded eyes nicks what's left of the grass along the river that flanks this town. Black flies shoulder up to the day lilies. Which brings me to the shack where you lived by the railroad tracks—always dusty—warming itself in the sun. Like a stone. And what of the signs we chose to ignore: the mare fallen on the road, its cast-off body overlooked; a boy crouching in the grass? So much is disappearing. I testify to what I see. Despite this hunger. Because of it.

Belye Nochi

Streets glazed with brine, the reek of a dead wren, and cabbage.

Midnight pearls down the narrow channels of Leningrad.

It is August. Moonless white nights skulk along the walk

to December Street. Further down, the boulevard and the bread-stand.

Our bodies are fugitive regrets: true morning will come

with its rusted sun scuffing the hide of our tongues.

Next year at this time no *syrniki* drenched in honey. No

candlelight or caviar. Not an apricot.

Akhmatova poses against a metal grate, a bandana at the neck of her

quarried words. At her feet, a bounty of stolen apples for the people.

At what cost this ripening thievery, feeding us in the wings

of a half-empty palace? The light from our mouths she was,

and was vapor that unleashed misfortune.

Occupying every room.

Teutophobia

    Entourage of mink coats/ chokers high hats/ of white wood orange peel/ of pearls rugs buttons in a cobalt jar/ of gabardine pale chambray/ of blue blood thin blood— gemmed vial for both— trinkets tassels shams and Schubert/ of all will: shrinking and ill will/ what's seen/unseen: the chiseled nettles: the exits the life-list the sudden tunnels/ the blade and socket/ the brew the breath the barefoot/ the swaddled/ the thin river that quickly deepened/ the shards of synagogues/ the synagogues/ the muscle/ of goosestep/ the wet leather of krystall/ of nacht/ of the accused/ and those who bowed/ the laid on fields of bone/ the stars/ boldened yellowed/ hung from the sky/

Oh/ Mother.

Estrangement—like sacrifice—begins as a word at first,

Estrangement: *to break up or breach, as in the valediction of the boy. As in you be my Rubicon.*

Birthright: *a false sense of security; the foolish logic of well-being.*

Loss: *low levels of albumin cause the heart to fail. Had he a heart, it was breached from birth. Comes from words meaning "failure to love."*

Shoplifting: *a handy crime; a fetal larceny. A slur.*

Fleecing: *a babe-in-the-woods breaks in on its own life blood. The soul is deaf to its own demise; as in could talk but won't; no parcel of legacy. No vestige of ancestry.*

Well: *also known as justly, deeply, a source, a fountainhead; a nod to the mineshaft or the verb to gush, as in the flow of blood or love*

Black Sea Port, 1941

I waved as if I knew them, though I did not. Only that they waved furiously to us on the pier. Dull-eyed, watching from below. They waved with the glee of the lucky few, their first small winnings hidden in coat seams; they held hands, raised tiny flags, wore overcoats and dresses, suits, scarves and hats, though it was spring. I felt afraid for all of us. The wind blew; caps and fedoras fell to us, like an offering, some slipping into the water, water the color of my husband's eyes. A persistent gray moving the ship further away. A passenger with a fiddle played and we hurried to the end of the pier. We waved. It gave us something to do. We needed to be close to those fleeing. We witnessed the tilt of our lives as if we were in steerage. But we were here, on shore, the evening sun behind us, our backs turned away, billows of smoke driving them further as we headed back to town where some were burning our shops, others coming for our homes.

My Father, Who Refused to Sit Shiva

We misunderstood our luck
growing up in that house —
third from the corner, where the forsythia

bloomed, as though to mock us, and my brothers hurried
down the street with a handful of bees in a jar,
for father who had a thousand demands,

who did not easily love, but was loved, who put the boys
in their place with a razor-tongue — afraid to let go of them,
yet keeping a distance — who lacked the know-how to father,

who struggled—feeling diminished in their world as they grew—
who held in his pocket the several sorrows of the world
when the boys got older and first one, then the other died.

My father, who refused to hold *shiva*, though he sat fixed
for a week beneath the shrouded mirror. Friends
came anyway, pressing against us like broken stalks

under an impossible weight, some hugging casseroles,
others with bouquets, surrendering the bare-throated
flowers, a continuous loop of murmured comforts

feeding the machine of our grief. So many things
disappear in the world: lilacs. Even the bending light
leaves, though the windows linger.

Unaccounted for, the long-numbered streets.
A river that once flanked our city.
And father, overwhelmed and immovable,

withdrew, watched as those who could leave, left
the wreckage of our home.

Elegy: Rehovot, Israel, 1984

.A string of water pearls hung from an urn, once
      retrieved from the Dead Sea by my Uncle Goel
who was killed years ago. Shot dead in his orchard
      by someone stealing the fruit. It was Shabbat.
On the night that followed his murder
      we all gathered at the pine table pulling leaves
from the Jaffa oranges he had grown and loved.
      The mirrors, which hung low, were covered.
Outside, white violets everywhere, suggesting
      the next task: laying him down.
In the slow days that followed the burial,
      much uncertain laughter.
We were hungry but could not confess to it.
      Darker still was what we should do now.
On the last day my father led the prayer in perfect Hebrew.
      Someone whistled in the kitchen and broke the spell.
No one took offense.
      Any one of us might have turned to leave,
but we were shoulder-to-shoulder
      where we stood in our sorrow and it seemed natural
to ask *what now*, of the salads, brown bread,
      bowls of citrus from the orchard edged in mint,
just-picked avocadoes dipped in lime juice,
      so we ate.

{The Crows of Dresden}

My mother dreaded anything with a beak. Eagles and doves no exception. When the windows were open and a house sparrow flew in, she ran. Ran for the door, the fields out front and the forest behind our house. The earth filled with feathers. My mother fretted. She shuddered with coughs. I ran to soothe her, but in her head, birds circled, flocks conspired. Any head-under-wing left Mother open-jawed: the raven, the hawk, even the black-capped chickadee, with its common *coo-coo*. I yelled for Father who came with a broom. Mother flailed her arms like a wide-winged fowl. I held her and whispered: *The black crows of Dresden are gone. The dark-beaked creatures on Hübner Strasse, picking at bits of Jews. The men in long coats and black boots marching on a street you once knew of as home. All gone.*

Mother of Rough Tongue

Mother of fibers and long feet, of high-brow and piano, of
      forte and lento and cabbage stuffed and plumped
      who once, rising from the grave took to throwing stones.

Mother of mine, whose mothering thread was bone on bone.
      Oh cross-bound, high-heeled, pearled at the opera.
      Oh mother of grimace and charm sailing across the sea,
      who stood knock-kneed, hate-whipped on the starboard side.

It was 1939, your family renegades from the Third Reich, your mother—
      mouth of brine—dodging you on deck, your doubts and dreads,
      the unshakable Atlantic backing you up. taking you home.

Oh mother of pedaled machines. Of pleats and shirrs and Schubert.
      Of thin-ribboned breath, of fretting and frenzy, your husband—
      your cousin—hidden in linens and chintz.

Mother who buried your first and second boys, of dashing out, disappearing
      in the high grass and blackberry shrubs. You with your quiver and panic
      and broken glass. Shocked-by-nothing. You were lovely even then, Mother.

Gleaned

The birds were feeding
                        and I swayed
like a pendulum   Blue
      November light poured from me

It was Thursday   My mother died
     her eyes   the color of a Brueghel field
I looked out one window   the great heart of earth
                      no longer beat
Moonless and close   I ate by the door   rose to be blessed
                                       on a quilt not my own
I had been bright fruit

unbroken until then.

A Lamenting

When I came home to bury her she had already been bathed—draped in white. According to custom we had to bury her within a day. It was January. Who would show in a cold that buried the city? I paid others to mourn my mother. I hired wild old mourners to wail. I leaned on them; 13 thin figures in buttoned-down fleece coats, short black boots, keening like distant spirits, letting me let go of the last thing on earth. Women with a gift. Continuous lamenting, hand wringing, tribal cries. A few pulled at their hair. Some softly wept and some sobbed in throaty ululations, said the unsayable in full howl, feigned a grief dedicated to my dear, my mother. I will remember her ushered out by the crying of strangers, widows who sobbed out of habit.

II.

Ancient Fall

In the beginning   hectares of weedy field   between thick woods
      the forests   the falls by a long lake   stained blue

What did I know   of the menace and flaw
    that would sweep through   this earliest garden?

How could I have   shouldered up   to the bark of a tree
    taken fruit from a limb   I could not reach   on my own?

Day was breaking   the world was hungry
     and I knew   that I'd be doubted   unforgiven

Taking from the tree   that shaped desire
        the tree   that put an end   to my wanting

There's Still the Fruit

Where he fucked me, I can't remember. His bed, but where I can't say. A brick house behind the thick smell of the camp. After hours of hauling stones I wanted to be touched. I had not yet eaten. Let the others in the background wheelbarrow themselves to another landscape. I bury them in my sleep. This is about what the living do to live. He was kind, with skin much like my own; with yellow hair like the faraway fields. He said his parents were teachers and that he loved to read. I listened to his stories as if I thought he'd ask questions afterwards. When he was done with me and the body I carried. Each night he'd lead me to a different room, in a building much like the others, where we sat a few moments on the balcony that overlooked thatched roofs and broken fences. One night, he pointed out a grove of flowering birches. Something I wouldn't have noticed from the barracks below. Then he led me inside to the bed and I let him undress me. Oh, the sorrow of those Sundays, when he looked at me and I looked calmly away. Let him. And he let my skin press against his and we touched and pulled back to look and I knew I'd never be anything more.

When he was done, he gave me an apple. An apple! And thanked me. And led me to wash over a basin on the floor.

Threadbare, We are Homesick

After the war the world is small again. Enough has survived to start a country. For miles, as far as the eye takes you, towns hardly alive tilt on the sand. Stopped trains wait for something to move them. The air is thick with worry. I search for a quartet in the town of my people but find no one except for a desperate boy pointing to my cello, which I hold onto, belly-down. It is my father as a boy. Who knows how, in the half-lit morning hours, people see what they long for? In this shadow world there is no father, just the slight weight of his memory, the almost-human moan of my cello, the ghostly groan seeking four chairs for a chamber, a night-song to hold me alone in this new republic. I am homesick, although I do not know where home is. But a faraway music holds my attention: the adagio I played years ago while Father sat for hours in his chair and hummed. An impressive audience, enough to fill the town, sits atop the moving trains, fanning themselves with their top hats and berets. On cue we open with an effortless *adagio* for strings whose middle-passage initiates a slight dynamic change to *andante*. Now listeners hold their hats. Hours pass but they do not stir, until dusk, with the roused *allegretto*, when they grow animated as though suddenly wound up, throwing carnations, shouting bravos. My father sits beside me playing his violin. We play on, losing ourselves in the earth's décor, our swaying bodies polished in the next sun, our tears pooling at the small scratch of our wood. Penniless, not broken, we move from town to town, appearing suddenly out of the dust. The same trains stand on their tracks. The same people wait as if to preserve the heartbeat. Ah, Mozart, man of loose buttons, the flustered nerve of the world taking up most of the sky. *Con affeto.*

This Season

This the year of
  empty boulevards, the sun dumbly shining—
    of gloved hands and masked mouths

the open stream closed for the season
  green parks yellow-taped
    throbbing in desert sun

Invisible along the selvage of our common cloaks
  along the footpaths, affixing themselves
    to the body of the world

This season we keep children close
  far from the objects within objects
    none of them human

Season of shortage & panic buying
  farmers dumping milk
    & plowing down crops

contagion
  demon-bred
    invisible, wedged

What are the body's limits
  when bane & burden
    strengthen as they shadow us

hanging on
  for hours or days
    until we ask *is it safe*

How do we tend to
  the system of things
    where is our bounty of seeds & salt

How do we stay kind & clean
    separate that which is
        good from the rest

Do we wait to be summoned
    & if so for how long this
        vestigial stain, our angling

for the washing of hands
    the washing of hands
        the wash

then the burning of
    the wiping away
        of everything else. Amen.

A Field Guide to Oświęcim, 2012

On the camp's   periphery
                        maculate   flowers
petals   blue with soil

the cleft earth   its rift
                     its depth   hand-troweled

How milky the lupine   which flourish nearby

               no pasture   birch bark   poplar   willow

a blade of grass   sepia light
Someone speaks   from my body:

      after the war   *the world is small*
              laced   *with bullet dust*

In a soft pile:
             the Kaufmann girl's hair
                coiled   in a chilly wind
oh ashen sun

They Filled with Promise and Worth

> *Invisible, indivisible Spirit,*
> *how is it you come so near*   -H.D.

Maker of the tender lamb/ of the nuns you marry in the courthouse of heaven/ Your young brides sing your song of our nation in the halls of justice/ Author of Schubert and the deep song of Góngora/ creator of Ruth and the widows— hear us/ architect of landscapes/ How do you sleep in skies swollen with our desperate faith/ Are you not our Father/ engineer of the windswept in the wilderness/ Lord of the tall men in winter coats setting fires starting ovens/ a record written on their bodies/ of the gathering migrants who lean into these fields where the swaddled, small as husks of corn/ burn/ Consider the things which dim and die in your grace/ gravity fleshing out those who linger too long in the dark garden of mausoleums/ What of the men and the boys who scale walls and jump when the fog lifts/ Carry them back/ The jittery the faint the fray-hemmed and flat-eyed/ lift them from hunger/ those who desire kingdom come/ those who gather their skirts to cross the river/ who forgive/ give birth while rising waters warn them/a sharp rock in their hands/ dogs barking in the birdless blood-red sky/ For almost any animal dead-ended at the sea or walled off at a crossing between lands/ bleeds out/ their dark poured into the very light you made/

If the muzzle of indifference

      gives to us hope,
should we?
If we hurry, if we mop up the mess of
      kitchen and country
we could emigrate and fresh-off-the-boat of our ignorance,
      be refugees, who, with arms
      open to receive, receive open-armed.
Remember the scene near the sea: tear gas,
      a diapered child held by the mother
      like a bundle as she ran toward the water? That.
That could be us if our first breath breathed
      were labored and we were hollow-boned poor.
      If the game of government saved
your faraway child from slow drowning, would you surrender?
      Would you save her, as water rushed into your open mouth?
How many in a boat of refugees and to whom do they belong?
      If, in a fresh state of fear your arrival point was
      anywhere but home,
where along the bankrupt avenues from here to there, would it be?
      If, at the end of a night everyone promised to meet again,
      would we mistake a thousand unbearable eyes for a lit road
and cross it?
If the eyes of a broken doll were glazed in death would you still
      buy it for your child. Any child?

Invocation

Unveil the lost among us. Feed us as you have in the good years. In the dark rift of this worried world, bring to us the last of the olive trees. In the workroom of night, lift up your satin sleeve. Smooth the edges where the dying have lain.

A River

Beyond the trees   a ghostly riverbank

    where children   once bathed

A river   where the gentle   dead are kept

Where is the everything

    I prayed for   a record written

        on the body

fallen at my feet   there

        beyond the trees

Epilogue

Dear Blood,

What we have here are bone songs
on the backs of children
who lullaby in the kennels

My busy hands busy filling bullets
Funeral mouths on fire
charms in the bottled hair

ash of fetus
ash of all
shadow-smoke

The blackbirds splay their wings
and poof! a dark shroud covers
the snowy earth

Take your stone and sling, love
Take my head in your hands

Lola Kaufmann, age 17
Birkenau barracks

Notes

Page 7 **Belye Nochi,** the White Nights are the luminous northern midsummer eves when the high latitudes are bathed in a pearlescent all-night glow in St. Petersburg. Anna Akhmatova lived in the Fontanka House, which was originally a country estate in the 1700's. After the revolution the house was nationalized.

Page 8 **Teutophobia,** meaning the fear of Germans or German things. My mother and her family fled Dresden, Germany, when she was 17 years old. She experienced the terror and panic of the Nuremburg Laws set in 1935 resulting in her dismissal from school, harassment, and her father's business was seized.

Page 14 {**The Crows of Dresden**} As a young girl in Germany, my mother experienced first-hand the trauma that the 3rd Reich unleashed. Years later, she still exhibited great fear of German Shepherds and birds. Mostly birds.

Page 19 **Threadbare, We are Homesick,** This is our world where art poses as the savior to humanity. This poem is for my father taught me how to listen to music. How to play, mimic the sound of a human voice.

Page 24 **A Field Guide to Oświęcim, 2012,** Auschwitz-Birkenau, where the present beauty and the historical horror collide. Many of my parents' relatives were killed at Auschwitz.

Page 28 **A River,** is referring to Babi Yar, a ravine in the Ukrainian capital Kyiv and a site of massacres carried out by Nazi Germany's forces during its campaign against the Soviet Union in World War II. The first and best documented of the massacres took place on 29–30 September 1941, in which some 33,771 Jews were murdered. Other victims of massacres at the site included Soviet prisoners of war, communists and Romani people. It is estimated that a total of between 100,000 and 150,000 people were murdered at Babi Yar during the German occupation.

Page 30 **Dear Blood,** my mother's cousin, from Będzin, Poland, was the only family member who survived Auschwitz-Birkenau. For 4 years she endured the camp. I lived with her in Israel. She left an astonishing account of her experience through the Shoah Foundation interviews.

About the Author

Carine Topal, born and raised in NYC, holds a MA from New York University. She has lived in Jerusalem, Israel, where she worked with Palestinian merchants and was also employed by the Office of Assimilation, working with the settlement of Moroccan Jews. Since 1982, she has anthologized the poetry of special needs children, participated in the grassroots organization California Poets in the Schools, was the Poet-in-Residence for the city of Manhattan Beach and Poet-in-Education for Manhattan Beach elementary schools. Carine has had the privilege of conducting poetry workshops at the VA Hospital in Los Angeles. She has been awarded residencies in the U.S. and Russia, is the recipient of numerous poetry awards and honors, including the Robert G. Cohn Prose Poetry Award and the Briar Cliff Poetry Award, Red Wheelbarrow Poetry Prize, and others. Her chapbook "Tattooed" won the Palettes and Quills Poetry Chapbook Contest. Topal's fifth collection, *In Order of Disappearance*, was published by the Pacific Coast Poetry Series in 2017. She lives in the Southern California desert and by the sea, where she leads poetry and memoir workshops.

www.ingramcontent.com/pod-product-compliance
Lightning Source LLC
LaVergne TN
LVHW041347080426
835512LV00006B/655